# 6 PILLARS

## OF THE
## LIFE MANAGEMENT
## SYSTEM

Simple Steps To Improve Your Life,
Do What You Love, Ignite Your Passion
And Make A Difference

## RAKESH MISHRA

Dedicated to anyone who has ever felt stuck in life and is searching for meaning.

# Disclaimer

This book is the result of a compilation of observations, experiences, and results achieved by a variety of experiments and practices in different areas of life by author Rakesh Mishra, which are called the six pillars of the life management system. The author bears no responsibility for any results of any kind, and the viewpoints in this book are his own.

The intention of this book is to share Rakesh's own life journey, which helped him overcome many adversities and achieve numerous goals that seemed impossible for a poor farm boy. He feels it's his moral responsibility to share his experiences with others through this book in order to provide motivation and inspiration to act and achieve their own success.

All attempts have been made to verify the information provided by this publication. Neither the author nor the publisher assumes any responsibility for errors, omissions, or contrary interpretations of the subject matter herein.

Neither the author nor the publisher assume any responsibility or liability on the behalf of the purchaser or reader of these materials. This book is written for entertainment purposes only. The views expressed are those of the author alone and should not be taken as expert instruction or commands. The reader is responsible for his or her future.

This book makes no guarantees of future success. However, by following the steps listed in this book, the reader has a much higher likelihood of achieving success.

The views and stats expressed in this book are based on the author's personal experiences and observations within the corporate world, working with clients, through education, learning from coaches, and in everyday life.

Some names and identifying details have been changed to protect the privacy of individuals.

# Table of Contents

# Foreword by Paul Brodie

*"You have something special inside you. Something you know. Something you do. Something you can teach. You are already an expert."* ~ **Robert Kiyosaki**

The quote above is a principal that I have lived throughout my life. Everyone has something wonderful to share with the world, and it is my privilege to help support Rakesh by writing a foreword for his first book.

In full disclosure, Rakesh is my client, and I have helped him with structuring this book and with the publishing and marketing of it. Rakesh has a wonderful story to share, and it is my privilege to help him. Health and wellness are the true riches in life (to paraphrase Mahatma Gandhi). This is something deeply personal to me because in 2011, I was close to 340 pounds and had multiple health issues to the point where my doctor said I would be dead in five years if I didn't get my act together.

Over the next year, I lost sixty pounds and did what only five percent of our population was able to do—I was able to keep the weight off. What was the secret of my transformation? I chose to eat less and move more and wanted to share both the victories and setbacks associated with losing weight. In 2015, I wrote my first book, *Eat Less and Move More.* It completely changed my life when it became my first bestseller.

Initially, I wrote my books to help people who were struggling with weight and to increase revenue for my speaking business. Then a funny thing happened that was completely unexpected...

Readers and fellow authors began contacting me and asking if I could help them get published. At the time, I had published my third bestseller called *Positivity Attracts*. The book was launched around Thanksgiving 2015 and was my biggest success yet. *Positivity Attracts* combined with my two other books brought me the first of many four-figure months in royalties. It also got the attention of many people who wanted to get published with a proven system.

I share this story because we all have struggles and successes, and writing a book is a great way to share that journey. In *6 Pillars of the Life Management System*, Rakesh covers health, wealth, family, career/business, social life, and spirituality. All six are my own personal pillars for living a wonderful life, as I am sure they are for you as well.

Rakesh has lived an amazing life, and I truly enjoyed reading his book and supporting him in his own author journey. He has many more books in the pipeline, and it was an honor to help him share his story with the world.

With gratitude,
Paul Brodie

Go to http://www.GetPublishedPodcast.com to grab your free book and to get more information about how we can help you share your story.

# Introduction

Welcome to my book, *6 Pillars of The Life Management System* (LMS); these six pillars are **Health, Wealth, Family, Career/Business, Social Life,** and **Spirituality**. My goal is to help you through these steps to develop mental toughness, which will help you deal with any emotional challenges that normally stop people from pursuing their dreams.

This book was written as a result of analyzing my own life and the lessons I learned and shared with my friends, students, and family members. The kind of life-transforming results they achieved were my inspiration to write this book so I could help a broader audience improve their lives.

Let me take you back to the initial journey of my life. I still remember it vividly. It was a hot summer in June in my village of about 300 people, and I was in my early teens. The village had no modern amenities like automobiles, telephones, or electricity.

As I looked around the village, I saw people with their two-wheeled wooden carts being pulled by bulls, horse-drawn carriages called tongas, and bicycles—these were the only modes of transportation. For most families in this village, farming was the only source of income, and that included my family.

On this hot summer day my mom gave me twenty

pounds of wheat to take to the mill about 2 km away, outside of the village. She gave me two quarters to pay for the grinding of the wheat. I put the packet of wheat on the carrier on the back of my bicycle.

As I pedaled my bike down those muddy and sandy trails on my way to the mill, I felt very frightened that I might lose those two quarters because if I did, Mom would literally beat me, as that had happened in the past. For my family, two quarters was a lot of money. Since I was not tall enough to ride the bicycle while sitting on the seat, I had to stand on the pedals. Because of that and the deep sand, my pedaling was quite jerky and the chances were good that those coins could fall out of my pocket.

As I rode through the deep sand, I could hear the jingle of the two quarters as they bounced around together in my pocket. Then, after a short time, I couldn't hear any jingling coming from my pocket. I reached into my pocket to check for the quarters, and that's when it happened—I lost my balance. The bike jerked to one side and I fell with it. The bike fell on top of me. So there I was, lying in the hot sand with my bicycle lying on top of me, and all I could think about was...where are my mom's quarters?

I told myself, *Rakesh, don't panic. Just start filtering through the sand and find those quarters. Just do your best.* For forty-five minutes I searched through that hot, dry sand looking for my mom's two quarters. I never did find them, but I did find some other things: a two-cent coin, some smooth, shiny rocks, a girl's hairpins, and a shirt button.

As I was kneeling with my bare legs and bare feet burning in the hot sand, I decided to try one last time to find the quarters, to no avail. As I searched through the sand that final time, my mind was racing. I felt terrified that Mom was going to beat me, and I found myself wondering how I might become rich. But I couldn't think of anything, and so I decided that I had to go home and tell Mom.

Suddenly I felt really excited and realized that after forty-five minutes of hard work, though I did not find the quarters, I did find so many other things that I was never aware of on that path, even though I used to walk it every day. So as the saying goes, always aim for the moon, and even if you miss you will land among the stars. From that day onward I started stretching beyond my comfort zone every day by setting big daily, weekly, monthly, and yearly goals without worrying about the outcome, as I had nothing to lose, and when you have nothing to lose, anything is possible.

# Chapter 1

# Health

*"I believe that the greatest gift you can give your family and the world is a healthy you." ~Joyce Meyer*

I love the above quote, and it's so true that the best gift we can give to ourselves, our family, our society, and the world is a healthy body, otherwise we become a burden to the system. At that point, rather than contributing to the world, we become mere consumers of the world and end up living meaningless, unmotivated lives without any purpose.

It's never too early or too late to take care of your health. A healthy body triggers healthy thoughts, which in turn trigger healthy feelings that trigger healthy actions, and all of this culminates in healthy results. In general, a healthy body is the most important pillar of all.

Today we have easy access to so many treatments, medications, and other kinds of resources to help us maintain healthy lives, but at the same time we have plenty of options and temptations for unhealthy living, so it's up to us to make the choice.

1

For a teenage boy or girl, health may not be a priority, as a young body is more likely able to self-recover, but that is not the case for a seventy-year-old person. Statistics tells us that once we turn thirty, we should start paying special attention to our physical fitness—thirty is something of a warning age to stop taking your health for granted. When we turn forty, we've hit a kind of "red alert" age, which can be referred to as the start of the pressure cooker years or midlife crisis. Here are some indicators of this time of life:

- *Bulging tummy*
- *Starting to lose your hair or a thinning hairline*
- *Loss of sexual desire*
- *Start finding faults everywhere*
- *Overall, life becomes less interesting*
- *Often think about the purpose and meaning of life*
- *Hairs start appearing everywhere*

Let's put some thought into why we call them the pressure cooker years. What is the root cause? In my own experience and from observing my coaching clients, friends, and family, I realized that mostly between the ages of forty and fifty, we experience tremendous financial pressure to fulfill the sudden increased need for money for a home mortgage, children's higher education, dream vacations, medical bills, a dream car, expensive clothing, keeping up with current fashion, peer pressure, children's other needs, etc. Often we have only one income or a combined moderate family income; on top of that, there's the fear of losing our job or business because of increased competition and difficulty keeping up to date with technological advancements.

2

I had no major health issues, but at the same time I was very casual about my health and had no disciplined eating or drinking habits, as well as almost no physical exercise. Everything changed when I lost my wife due to complications that developed during a C-section delivery. She left me with two sons, ages three years and three hours old. My whole world collapsed; in fact, I decided to commit suicide that night in the hospital, but one thought changed my decision, which I will cover later in the Family Pillar.

With my increased stress and anxiety, one day I felt so dizzy I drove to a clinic, where the doctor found I had high blood pressure reading 180/110, so he put me on medication. This was the first time I realized that I was not young anymore and had silently slipped into midlife crisis. Regardless, I had a responsibility to raise two kids, plus I still had lots of life ahead of me with countless dreams and aspirations. I was determined to make drastic lifestyle changes to enable me to live a healthy life.

I am going to share my lifestyle changes as well as some of my own theories for healthy living throughout this chapter.

## Mishra 888 Sleep Theory

It's a simple practice I follow, and many of my clients, family members, and friends started using it with great results. Between 8:00 p.m. and 8:00 a.m., sleep for any eight hours with one condition—go to bed every day at the same time. The ideal sleeping window is between 9:00 p.m. and 5:00 a.m.

3

# Simple Solutions for Healthy Living

As I mentioned in the disclaimer section, I am not a health expert, but I am sharing with you what I practice in my own life. My ideas may or may not help you, so please consult the appropriate expert before practicing or applying any of the teachings in this book.

There are many areas of our lives where we need to be careful about healthy living, but the following are the three areas to which we need to pay particularly close attention. It's pretty simple to maintain a healthy body, but sometimes we make it complicated.

## Mental Health

Mental illness is increasing at an alarming rate these days and becoming a real challenge to our society, especially in the western world. There are many reasons for mental illness, and of course consulting with experts and getting treatment through medication and therapy is the standard practice. Though all ages are affected, lifestyle changes at an early age can help in a big way to improve mental health and create engaged living. Loneliness, for example, is one of the main contributing factors to mental illness, and it can be managed easily through a simple lifestyle change of engaging ourselves in more creative activities. Here are a few simple habits that can help you stay mentally fit.

- *Meet one stranger a day and leave him/her with a smile*
- *Read a book on an interesting topic*
- *Start some kind of movement and be actively involved in it*
- *Learn one new skill a month*
- *Engage in social media and add some value*
- *Take up volunteer assignments for a social cause*
- *Start writing about your life or try some creative writing*
- *Engage in some brain-stimulating exercises/activities*
- *Engage in some relaxing exercises like yoga and meditation*
- *Form a social group either online or offline and play an active part*
- *Get enough sleep—eight hours is ideal*
- *Write down and revisit happy moments from your past*
- *Help someone by making a difference in their life*

## Physical Health

Modern-day living, with its many technological advancements and automation, has made life so passive that we hardly get a chance to move our bodies, and we end up leading a sedentary lifestyle. This causes many illnesses, and if they're not cured in a timely manner, they can turn into chronic diseases, often resulting in life-threatening situations that could have been easily prevented with a few lifestyle changes. Here are some practices that I follow:

5

- *Go to the gym at least three days a week*
- *Thirty minutes of daily morning meditation; even one minute is a good start*
- *Drink two liters of water every day*
- *No alcohol consumption at all*
- *Get eight hours of sleep (follow the 888 Mishra Sleep Theory)*
- *No smoking*
- *No substance abuse*

The above practices will help you as they did me and can be altered based on your individual needs and circumstances. For example, going to the gym can be replaced with a walk or yoga. Alcohol and smoking can be reduced in the beginning and then slowly stopped.

The following three **M**s also can be very effective to improve our physical health.

**M**ind: Our mind is a reservoir of thoughts, and the kinds of thoughts we put into our mind are critical to our well-being. Our circumstances trigger our thoughts, thoughts trigger our feelings, feelings trigger our actions, and our actions determine our results. That means that controlling our circumstances becomes very important in order to control the thoughts in our mind, which in turn decide our results. So let's mind our mind, which is the mastermind of our results, which decide our life.

**M**outh: As we have seen in the case of the first M (mind) above, the kinds of thoughts we feed our mind decide our life; similarly, the kind of food we feed our mouth decides the condition of our gut. The gut plays a very important role in our well-being. Modern medical reports state that the gut is the central control for most of the diseases that threaten us. Simple food allergy and microbiome tests can be done to control our gut.

Food consumption habits can create drastic change to our health. Here are five such simple food habits:

1- *Reduce overall food consumption to half*
2- *Make half your meal portion salad and vegetables*
3- *Reduce each meal portion to half*
4- *Limit your eating time to ten hours, i.e., between 9:00 a.m. and 7:00 p.m.*
5- *Consume only warm/hot water, a big NO to cold/fridge water*

As they say, staying away from the following four evil white food items can be a tremendous help to improving your health. If you cannot avoid them, at least reduce the quantity of consumption and slowly stop completely; this might have magical results.

1- *Salt*
2- *Sugar*
3- *Flour*
4- *Rice*

Movement: Our modern lifestyle has many luxuries, which has led to sedentary living. We can still safely enjoy these luxuries if we add some movement to our body's routine on a daily basis. This can be achieved simply by joining a gym, using stairs rather than elevators, doing yoga, running on a treadmill, or walking outside.

Daily five-minute body movement exercises can bring a big health boost to our body. Here are the five different easy exercises, each taking only one minute, which will take care of moving all our major body parts. Search YouTube for more details or for ideas of how to add on to these exercises.

1. *Minute 1: Straight-leg deadlift*
2. *Minute 2: Add bicep curls*
3. *Minute 3: Add lunges*
4. *Minute 4: Add an overhead press*
5. *Minute 5: Add pushups*

**Bonus Exercise**: The most effective and complete exercise, which covers all the joints and muscles in your body, is the Sun Salutation.

## Emotional Health

Although all three health areas—mental, physical, and emotional—are intra-connected and impact each other, their individual control can be really effective for our overall health and well-being. Uncontrolled emotional health can badly impact our mental health, which in turn

8

can cause poor physical health. Emotional health is very sensitive and often difficult to diagnose, so it needs to be taken care of delicately. Developing thick-skinned thinking, often called developing mental toughness, helps our emotional health. As I mentioned, mental health experts can provide help, but on a day-to-day basis we can practice a few approaches that will help us to make our emotional health much stronger and healthier. Here are a few such habits, which come from a great book called *The Four Agreements* by Don Miguel Ruiz.

1. ***Don't take anything personally***
2. ***Don't make assumptions***
3. ***Always do your best***

In addition to the above three habits, here are two bonus habits that can be really effective in developing mental toughness.

**Expectation**: Try not to have any expectations from anybody—this will set you free and help you avoid emotional distress. Often our expectations lead to emotional breakdowns, which then lead to our unhealthy emotional condition. If you want to do a favor for someone or help someone, do it without expecting anything in return. Be especially careful when dealing with your close family members and close friends.

**Comparison**: Expectation and comparison are cousins, so do not compare yourself with anybody on anything in your life, as you are unique and you have your own gifts and skills to share in this world. Just live your life on your

9

own terms; it's fine to get inspiration from others' lives, but do not compare yourself to them because it will only lead to disappointments that will then lead to emotional distress.

As I mentioned, these are the habits I practice, and I have experienced their positive impact and curative effect, which helped me live a happy life with full emotional balance. That is the reason I am sharing my own experiences. They may or may not have the exact same effect for you, but they are sure to help. Remember, our time on Earth is limited, and each of us is playing our role, so there is no need to take life so seriously. Just live one day at a time and face and manage one challenge at a time.

## Emotional Health and Happiness-Anchoring Exercise

Think of your body as a boat in the middle of a lake with many anchors attached to it. No matter how hard we paddle, it's difficult to move the boat. We are no different than this poor boat because we have so many negative thoughts, which I call "Devil Anchors", that stop us from moving forward in our lives. We worry all day long, and soon we end up depressed, feeling exhausted and unmotivated. Here are two anchoring exercises that will help us live a happy and healthy life.

10

# Find Your Devil Anchors

Find some quiet place and spend thirty minutes to an hour writing down everything you worry about on a daily and weekly basis. Think of all the things that consistently drain your energy or make you feel anxious, and jot them down. Don't go into too many details, just write down five to ten words for each item. For example, fear of being sick, family well-being, financial trouble, losing a loved one, etc. This exercise can be scheduled at regular intervals until you get your life on track.

Once you finish the above exercise, look back at your list. There are probably a couple of things that really stand out as your top sources of worry and stress. Underline or highlight these two or three top Devil Anchors so you can deal with them in the next step.

# Remove Your Devil Anchors

Now take your first anchor from the above list and ask the question "How can I eliminate this Devil Anchor?" Write down the three simplest possible solutions. You may want to seek the help of your family, friends, or experts at some point, but try not to consult them at this stage. For example, if you worry about being lonely, you can find friends, engage online, or join meet-up groups—these are a few simple solutions.

After you write down three potential solutions for each anchor, then start applying them one by one, starting with

11

the simplest one and continuing through all three solutions one at a time. It may not completely resolve the worry or stress, but you will feel much more in control of your negative emotions than before, and that in itself is a big success.

The best part is that doing this exercise engages your mind, keeping it so busy that you do not have time to worry about your negative Devil Anchors.

As you'll see me mention many times throughout this book, I am not an expert or healer, I am just sharing my own practices with you. You may need to consult an expert before making changes to your lifestyle, but these exercises made a big difference for me, and I am more than happy to share them with you. Chances are these practices will bring positive results to you as well. Good luck.

**Book Recommendation**: **The Miracle Morning** *by Hal Elrod*

**Resource Guide**:
*https://www.CoachRakesh.com/WorkBookLMS*

# Chapter 2

# Wealth

*"When you have nothing, anything is possible."*
*~Dan Miller*

Money becomes just another form of oxygen for our survival. We often hear the phrase, "money is not everything", but the only people who make this statement are those who have accumulated wealth. Wealth is an integral part of our life right from birth to the very last day of our existence.

Money provides us the options and opportunities to live our lives in a comfortable way. As "Maslow's Hierarchy of Needs" indicates, once we meet our basic needs, we tend to move from consumer mode into contribution mode; for that to happen, wealth plays a very important role.

We are always seeking transformation from one stage to another. Based on the amount of wealth we have, we fall into the following three stages of transformation:

- *Survival*
- *Success*
- *Significance*

**Survival**: This is when we are able to fulfill our basic needs of food, shelter, and clothing and up to a certain level of safety and security. Unfortunately, approximately seventy to eighty percent of the world population falls into this category. To move to the next level, we need certain wealth.

**Success**: The definition of success is different for everyone based on their needs and desires—it could be a big house, good car, good health, good schooling for kids, good bank balance, funds for a special occasion, or a smooth retirement. We need lots of money to live successfully, but hardly ten percent of the world's population is able to afford this type of lifestyle. Wealth plays a very important role here.

**Significance**: Once someone moves from Survival to Success, they begin craving a higher meaning; in other words, they may start looking for the meaning and purpose of life. At the Survival and Success levels, you focus on yourself and/or your loved ones—often your family members—but you are still in consumer mode. When you use your existence on this planet as well as your products and services to start uplifting others' lives who may not be from your community, tribe, race, or religion. It's at this point that you start living at the Significance level.

There are many examples of people who fall into this category, like Mother Teresa, Nelson Mandela, Gandhi, Martin Luther King, and many more.

Since we all strive to live WORRY-FREE and leave REGRET-FREE, wealth is an equally important factor that enables you to transform your life as well as the lives of others. It also helps you build your legacy and as a result, you have the opportunity to live your purposeful life.

An abundance of wealth eliminates many insecurities, creates recognition in society, and provides options that add value to your life. In addition, you can get involved with and support your chosen causes—wealth often plays a very important role in this.

The following are examples of negative actions and issues often created by a lack of wealth:

- *Divorce*
- *Drug trafficking*
- *Terrorism*
- *Murder*
- *Gun crime*
- *Financial fraud*
- *People fleeing their own birth lands*
- *Lack of education*
- *Lack of food and water*
- *Poor job market*
- *Many health issues*

All third world countries are stuck with their "third world" status because there is a lack of wealth. This is getting worse by the day and creates many types of stress, from individual stress to financial stress, experienced by companies or countries.

15

There was a time when individuals went bankrupt, which in turn caused some companies to go bankrupt, and now we are living in a time when even whole countries are going bankrupt. A recent example is Greece.

If we take a closer look, we can see that this happens because of a lack of wealth, which proves my point that wealth plays a very important role at an individual level as well as the level of a corporation or organization, or for that matter, even a country. But that doesn't need to be the case—there is a way out of this dilemma that offers full control over wealth, which I will cover later in this chapter.

I'll use my own example to illustrate my point. I was a poor farm boy from India who didn't even start learning the English alphabet until the mature age of sixteen. One day while working with laborers in rice fields, I saw a flying object in the sky and made up my mind that someday, I would board that machine. Up to that point, the only forms of transportation I had used were the bullock cart and a bicycle.

However, I used to feel scared to even think about it because of my lack of wealth. One fine day everything changed, and a seed was planted in my mind to overcome this lack of wealth issue. I will cover this in the next section of the chapter.

## MY STORY

I'm going to take a moment to reflect on my own life here. My very first memory relating to wealth goes back to my time as a poor seven-year-old farm boy in a tiny, remote village of India. As I mentioned earlier, my village had no connection to any modern amenities: no automobile, no telephone, no electricity, and of course, no television. The only modes of transportation were bicycles and the two-wheeled wooden cart pulled by bulls. So when I became relatively wealthy in the mid 1980s, I brought the car, telephone, electricity, and television to my village for the very first time.

An aunt of mine used to live in both Dubai and the USA, and whenever she visited our village, we kids would surround her, fascinated by her expensive belongings. She would give us some change as a gift, which was a lot of money for a poor kid like me, so we could buy candies, but I always refused to accept it. I would go home crying and asking my mom why my aunty was giving us money—was it because we were poor? No, she'd say, she just loves kids.

I used to ask Mom why we didn't have that kind of money. Mom would explain that my aunt lived in Dubai and the USA, and that was why she was wealthy and could afford to give money away. I then asked my mom what Dubai and America were, but she said she had no idea if Dubai and America were countries or cities either inside or outside of India. For some strange reason this planted the idea in my mind that if I wanted to be wealthy, I'd have to get this thing called Dubai or America.

17

To make a long story short, it took almost twenty-five years before I finally went to Bahrain and Dubai as a sales and service engineer. Finally, during Y2K (the late '90s), I landed a job as an IT professional in San Francisco, California, USA, and I felt as if my life had truly began. But soon I realized that the Green Card process would be quite lengthy, so I decided to migrate to Canada instead. I moved there, was happily married, and had my first baby boy.

I became wealthy enough that I felt I had passed the Survival and Success levels; I then began seeking the significance of life, but I wasn't sure how to find my purpose. At the same time I was quite happy, content that at least my wealth allowed me to live worry-free; however, I wouldn't be able to leave the world without regret if I continued living at the Success level and didn't pursue Significance.

It was my thirty-fifth birthday, and some of my friends came to celebrate with me. We had cake, drinks, and food, but I couldn't sleep that night. I kept thinking that I was already thirty-five and before I knew it, I would be seventy, eighty, ninety, or even one hundred if I was lucky enough to live that long; then I'd be dead and gone. The next morning I woke up and told my wife, two-year-old son, and parents that I wanted to go to Cuba to find the purpose of my life. I chose Cuba because I was curious about visiting a country that had no major support from the rest of the world. In other words, similar to my experience growing up in India, this country had no connection to modernity, and most people lived in poverty yet were still happy. I could relate to this country, so it was the perfect place to spend some

18

quiet time reflecting on my own life and purpose.

In a few weeks I was in Cuba, where I became used to getting up late in the morning with a hangover, taking a few dips in the ocean, then going back to my hotel and having a couple of beers. I would lie down on soft white towels and write; I wrote 1,700 pages in one week, and when I reread what I'd written, to my surprise I realized that I was happiest when I was helping others reach their potential. I decided to become a billionaire—of course not in dollar terms, but rather I wanted to reach out to a billion people and help them by influencing them positively in some way before my last breath.

The next issue I faced was that before helping others, I had to support my family in Canada as well as in India. I had limited wealth, which was not enough to carry out my passion to positively influence a billion people.

Then I asked myself a question: What did I need in order to become financially free so that I could fulfill my billionaire dream? I decided that it came down to three things, and if I could achieve them in the next ten years and retire at forty-five, then I could spend my time fulfilling my billionaire purpose. The three things I needed to accomplish were:

- *Pay off my home loan*
- *Put $100,000 aside for each of my children for their education*
- *Find some way to have a passive earning of $5,000 per month*

I did a rough calculation—I would need $2,500,000 to achieve my forty-fifth birthday retirement dream so that I would be able to live my purpose and passion.

I came back to Toronto, worked a full-time job, and after some research, I decided to do consulting work and then open a placement agency parallel to my job. This, in addition to all the extra savings from real estate investments (luckily in and around Toronto, real estate did very well), meant I was going to reach my $2.5 million goal well before my forty-fifth birthday.

Finally I felt that I was wealthy and could do anything I desired. Happy and fulfilled, I started reaching out to people to help them through my speeches and social media platforms.

All of sudden there was a twist in my life—my wife delivered a second baby boy, but she passed away on the hospital bed due to some complications developed from the C-section. My life took a 180-degree turn and I was totally devastated. After some soul-searching, I came to grips with the fact that I couldn't change what had happened, so I had to focus on what could I do now.

It took almost three and a half years before I decided to marry for the second time; during that time I was raising my babies but felt like life had slowed down. I found my soul mate in India and life once again started moving ahead. When my second wife gave birth to my third son, my life seemed to become fully functional once again. Of course, there were many challenges, but my accumulated wealth played a vital part in reconstructing my family life; I will cover this in great detail in the next section of this chapter.

## REASON

Although my life included many challenges, my wealth accumulation gave me the confidence that allowed me to continue with my life plan and share my struggles with others in order to give them the confidence to move with life's flow. Despite facing adversities as bad as losing my better half, I still hoped that I could achieve my goals and raise my kids in a fully responsible way.

Through all my hardships and the chaos in my life, I learned an important lesson, which gave me an *aha moment* as well as the following message that I want to share with the world:

"No matter how bad and adverse the situation is, as long as you are breathing, it's not done yet! And once you stop breathing, who cares."

So just keep stretching beyond your comfort zone, and find and live the purpose of your life before your beautiful life journey comes to an end. That's what I did, and my wealth accumulation helped me live my purpose by giving me confidence and allowing me to take risks even when I was not experiencing any financial gains. It allowed me to take chances.

21

After tasting so many successes and facing so many failures, the lesson I learned that gave me another *aha moment* was:

**"Failures always add CONFIDENCE, success always creates INSECURITY."**

I learned this and felt with all my heart that the real secret to success is: Fail fast! Fail often! Fail early!

***"Fail as big as you can afford, that is the key to real SUCCESS!"*** This was only possible because my accumulated wealth gave me the freedom to not only fail but to FAIL BIG, and that's what I did. I still continue doing this on a continuous basis.

At that point, I was living my life at the Significance level and started to reflect on my childhood passions. I figured out that I loved public speaking, and I had countless stories to share with the world. However, I was feeling a bit hesitant because I was worried that if I shared my stories of struggle and poverty, people may not like me. Then one day I saw the movie *Slumdog Millionaire*, and after watching it I realized that I had lived almost eighty percent of that story, which meant I should share my own stories—people would like them, and I may even win an Oscar (figuratively!).

I loved public speaking, but I also had a fear of it. One day while having coffee at the Ministry of Transportation office where I used to work as an IT consultant, I saw an advertisement for Toastmasters. I just walked into their meeting room as a guest, and after attending a few meetings became a regular member. That's how I began developing my public speaking abilities so that I could motivate  and inspire audiences from all possible stages whenever I got the chance to speak.

I started listening to the great Jim Rohn's audiobooks, in which he talked about the following two secrets, which can help you achieve abundance in any walk of life.

- ***You are the average of the five people you spend most of your time with***
- ***You should invest five percent of your income on your self-development***

This brought on another *aha moment*, and my wealth accumulation once more helped me dive into a new area of self-development. I invested in myself by hiring speaking coach Steve Lowell for one year in 2017, which helped turn me into a very confident speaker. In addition, he helped me polish and structure my speeches.

Through Jim Rohn's teachings, I realized that my current friends were not doing very well, and it was time to move on to choose a new friends circle. I discovered a website called www.canada411.com, which helps you find a person or business, so I just put a common Indian last name into the search, along with the city where I was looking for friends, primarily in and around Toronto. To my surprise, 252 potential contacts popped up! I called them and met thirty-six of them one-on-one as well as fourteen families, whom I invited to my house. They became my "certified

23

friends"—I had used fifteen conditions to shortlist these friends while interviewing them over the phone.

Now at this point, I had learned how to face adversities, build wealth, master public speaking, make influential friends, and develop skills that could help me build my wealth. In short, I became a master at how to transition from Survival to Success to Significance and started mentoring my friends and their friends for free because my wealth accumulation allowed me to do so.

Soon I realized that I had an even bigger purpose, and I needed to explore beyond Canada and India. I started watching motivational videos, buying and reading books, and attending conferences, and I realized that something new was happening that would impact the world—the people who would be in great demand were those who could solve other people's problems. Since much of the information you need to learn is available for free, what will make a difference in somebody's life and make you stand out is soft skills like public speaking, using communication skills to manage people, and becoming a problem solver by learning the needed skills in the marketplace.

## IMPACT

By this time I had complete confidence that I could achieve any goals I desired. In fact, anyone can achieve his/her goals if they follow the steps described below. Your mindset needs to embrace the following two things:

- *Unwavering faith*
- *Extraordinary effort*

In terms of financial/wealth goals, you just need to learn two things in order to achieve them:

- *How to set them*
- *How to achieve them*

## How to Set Goals

You can set your goals by using the following SMART formula.

**S:** Specific – Your goal has to be specific. Just saying you want to earn lots of money is not specific, but saying you want to earn $200,000 by the end of the calendar year *is* specific.

**M**: Measurable – Your goal has to be measurable. If your goal is to become beautiful, can you really measure that? Or if your goal is to be happy, again, can you measure it? But if you say that you want to lose twenty pounds in the next twelve weeks, YES, you *can* measure it.

**A**: Attainable/Achievable – Your goal should be justifiable and attainable. Saying "I want to live 200 years" is not attainable. But YES, you can set a goal that nobody has yet achieved that you feel you can. There are many such examples, like the invention of the airplane. More realistic goals, like wanting to become a millionaire in next the three years, are attainable—YES, you can.

25

**R**: Realistic – Your goal should be realistic. A goal to become president of the United States of America when you're Canadian is not a realistic goal.

**T**: Time-bound – Your goal should have a time limit or deadlines. You can say you want to save $50,000 but by when—in the next six months, six years, or in your lifetime? But if you say you want to save $50,000 in the next twenty-four months, now your goal has a deadline and makes more sense.

So far we've learned how to set these goals following the above SMART formula, which will make it much easier for you to achieve them. Now let's talk about *how* to achieve these goals.

This is the five-step process you can use to achieve any goal you set for yourself. Remember, before following the five-step process below, your goal should satisfy the SMART formula test.

## How to achieve goals

Use the following five-step WWWRF formula to achieve any goal:

1. *What do you want*
2. *Why do you want it*
3. *Who has achieved it*
4. *Reach out to the person in step #3 or read his/her teachings and execute them*
5. *Find some accountability partners to work with*

## What do you want?

Clarity is king! Once you clarify exactly what you want, that becomes the goal you'll work toward.

## Why do you want it?

Knowing why you've set this goal is very important because the stronger your desire is to achieve it, the easier it will be to reach it and any goal you want. Normally it has to be beyond only serving yourself and often falls into the Significance level; this usually has something to do with your passion and purpose in life. But at the same time, it can be as simple as paying off your debt.

## Who has achieved it?

If somebody else has already achieved the same goal, why can't you achieve it too? And if nobody has done it before and you're able to accomplish it, that is the real doing. Chances are that whatever you want to achieve, someone else has already done it and probably wrote a book, has an online course, or some other way you can access his/her teaching of the steps or process he/she used to achieve success. Now it's your turn to do the same.

## Reach out to the person who has achieved it

Once you know who has already achieved your desired goal, contact that person or access his/her teachings in whatever form they may be—speeches, courses, books,

27

mastermind programs, group programs, etc. Then prepare a system that involves all the necessary steps to achieve your desired results. Simply execute these steps, correcting and modifying them as needed by following the just-in-time learning philosophy. And don't forget to enjoy the journey!

## Find an accountability partner

This step is the most important, because if you are not held accountable to someone during your goal-reaching process, which can be quite a lonely journey, there is a higher chance that you will give up or get distracted. So always either hire a coach/mentor or work with a friend who is also working on their own goal, and you can become accountability partners for each other.

It's up to you how you want to create wealth—you can use other people's money (in the form of loans) to start your business faster, or you may have a problem-solving skill that people are willing to pay for. Just identify this product or service and follow these two steps for your wealth freedom:

1. **Apply the SMART formula to set your financial goals**

2. **Apply the five-step WWWRF formula to achieve your goals**

*Book Recommendation*: *I Will Teach You To Be Rich* by Ramit Sethi

*Resource Guide*:
https://www.coachrakesh.com/WorkBookLMS

# Chapter 3

# Family

*"Family is not an important thing, it's everything."*
**~Michael J. Fox**

Our family is an institution in which we often deal with three to five generations at a time: our grandparents, parents, ourselves, our children, and our grandchildren. **Relationships** are the common threads that hold this institution together. It's never been so challenging to deal with relationships as in the last twenty-five years, especially since the beginning of the year 2000. The world did not experience as much change in the last 200 years as it has in last twenty-five years, especially after the invention of the Internet.

The entire fabric of the family has been redefined, and emotional bonds among families have been largely overtaken by the practical approach of life. People started enjoying their independence, and as a result, fewer and fewer people now believe in marriage and instead are opting to stay single or are simply living together without the benefit of marriage. More and more, divorces and broken families are becoming the norm, tearing apart the family support system, and as result, loneliness is on the rise. This has become the main cause of depression, anxiety, mental illness, and so many other chronic diseases.

30

There is no point in becoming wealthy and healthy if your family is falling apart as a result, so from that perspective, out of the six pillars of the LMS, the family becomes one of the most impactful pillars of all. I would like to share the story of one of my clients, which will reveal many hidden nuances of the family as an institution and how important it is to maintain this pillar in the best possible way.

After I had given a presentation at momondays Brampton, a gentleman came up to me and congratulated me on my speech. I felt very touched; he then gave me his business card and asked for my phone number. The next day he called me and we met for lunch, which lasted for four hours. He explained his situation and I gave my views on the subject, which he appreciated. He became emotional and told me that he found me to be a great guide/teacher/mentor, and I told him that I was able to help him because I had also gone through similar situations and had heard many other comparable stories from friends and loved ones.

This gentleman was involved in many successful businesses, but all his time was dedicated to business; he never had time to spend with his children, wife, and parents. This was revealed when I asked him when he last went on a family vacation, and his response was "never" even though he was almost fifty-five years old. However, he said that he did go on vacation with his male friends. I asked him where his wife was, and he told me she had gone to Germany to visit her brother. I then asked him when her birthday was, and he said it was in ten days.

31

I asked him if he could surprise his wife by going to Germany and taking her to Switzerland to celebrate her birthday, which would also make up for the honeymoon they never had. He became emotional and said that would really surprise his wife and make her happy, and he started crying. In the end, he did go to Germany and took her to Switzerland for a week. His wife told him that she would like to talk to his newfound mentor, Rakesh Mishra; when she spoke to me, she invited my family and me over for dinner when she got back to Toronto.

It was my very first time meeting this man's family, and I decided to go by myself. When I reached his home that evening, I discovered that he had also invited seven other couples whom he had told great things about me. I found myself among sixteen men and women and the only person I knew was my friend, who had become my client. My friend asked if I would please mentor all seven couples the way I mentored him during our four-hour lunch, and I explained that that was his personal situation and everyone's situation is different, but I would be more than happy to help them, which I did.

After the dinner, as I was about to leave, my friend got a little emotional—he had drunk a bit too much. He took out his checkbook, handed me a blank check, and asked me to fill in a reasonable amount for my coaching fee. He said he knew how to make lots of money, but I had taught him how to live a balanced life and especially a happy family life. I turned down his offer and told him that we would talk about it later, but he was adamant and wrote a check for $10,000, which he offered to me. I saw the amount and turned it down, then took his checkbook and wrote $1,997 on a check, asked him to sign it, and that was my first ever paid coaching client. Later on, all seven families became paying clients.

By the end of 2018, I had coached sixty-three couples, all referred to me through word of mouth. Most of my potential clients contact me by phone and some via email, which they get from my existing clients. I send them ten questions to answer, which they have to send me a week before we meet for our five-hour coaching session. Normally I book a small conference room in a hotel for six hours, mostly between 9 a.m. to 3:00 p.m.

Based on their responses to the ten questions, I prepare my interview questions in advance. When we meet at 9:00 a.m., we start by signing the contract, and then I explain the process. The actual session starts at 10:00 a.m. sharp. I begin by chatting with the couple for two hours while I take notes, and if they agree, I record the conversation to refer to afterward. Then we break for lunch at noon for one hour.

We resume the session at 1:00 p.m., at which time I speak to them individually for thirty minutes each. In the final hour I explain the solution to them and answer any questions they may have. I also tell them that I will be sending them a complete step-by-step action plan in PDF format and offer them a free thirty-minute Zoom or phone consultation, which they would need to use within the next 100 days.

33

Until the end of 2018, I was charging $1,997 for this five-hour couples coaching; starting January 1, 2019 my fee increased to $2,497, and I also offer a 10 percent referral bonus for existing clients.

The reason I shared this information is because after coaching more than sixty-three couples, I realized that in order to lead a happy life, out of all of the six pillars, Family has been the most important pillar, yet we often take family for granted and end up living unfulfilled lives. By the time we realize this, it's too late.

In today's world, both parents work, there is no job security, and due to technological advancements, we're always feeling pressured to upgrade our technology on a regular basis. In the workplace, the younger generation is preferred over older employees, and day by day, things are getting harder and harder for job seekers. With the introduction of robotics, artificial intelligence, and virtual reality, things are really getting tough in the workplace, especially for job seekers.

Often the pressures of the office enter our homes, which creates quite a stressful situation. Family members hardly get the chance to spend any quality time with each other, and in many cases, these situations spiral out of control and often end up in divorce or some other unpleasant habits like alcohol, drugs, gambling, extramarital affairs, and other serious issues. In most of the broken families where relationships are falling apart and situations end in divorce, the following factors are mainly responsible:

- *Financial crisis*
- *Sex*
- *Communication gaps*
- *Other people's involvement*

Often social pressure also becomes a factor in people's family life—we find ourselves in a race to keep up with others and never get a chance to really analyze our own situation and act accordingly. If we focus on ourselves, we can discover the opportunities that are available today— we are living in one of the best times ever to easily avail ourselves of the avenues for financial gains. But in order to do that, we need to add discipline to our lives; sit down and identify the problematic areas of your life, then reach out to the appropriate experts for a solution.

To make the Family Pillar really strong, relationship management becomes critical and is very easy to maintain with a little effort. However, you need to change your attitude and utilize the following relationship builders in your day-to-day dealings with family members.

- *No ego*
- *No expectations*
- *No comparisons*
- *"Let go" approach*
- *Don't take things personally*
- *Don't make assumptions*
- *Practice rather than preach approach*
- *Encouragement approach*

35

- *Admit mistakes where appropriate*
- *Avoid finding fault with others*
- *Make your point very clear*
- *Say it rather than holding a grudge*
- *Empathetic approach*
- *Practice smiling*
- *Allow them to express their perspectives*

Based on my own family life and the types of practices and habits I follow, I have come up with a Happy Family Living Formula, which requires you to dedicate just thirteen hours out of 8,760 hours in a year. Here is how to implement this formula.

## Step #1

Decide the date and time each month—for instance, on the fifteenth of every month at 7:00 p.m.—and have every member of the family gather in a common place for one hour. Family members living in other cities or countries can join through video chat.

Now divide sixty by the number of family members participating in the meeting to determine how much time each person has to speak. For instance, if there are ten family members, you would divide sixty by ten, which equals six, so each person would have six minutes to speak or share his or her side. If you want, you can draw names to decide the speaking order. Once the meeting gets started, everyone will share the following three things in the first three minutes, then in the remaining three minutes, family members can provide their comments, support, help, and feedback.

1. *How did last month go? Share wins and what went well.*
2. *What current challenges are you facing? Do you need any help?*
3. *What commitment you are going to make for next month?*

The same three steps must be completed by each member of the family. The best part is that everybody gets the chance to express his or her challenges and wins. You can then customize these meetings by doing things like celebrating the wins and deciding on accountability partners.

You can play fun games or do some other activities to make these monthly meetings more like a celebration, which will help build strong relationships among family members. After all, family happiness is all about strong relationships.

I have been implementing these exercises for ten years, and I introduce them to every coaching client of mine. They simply love it and are getting tremendous results. You could also consider dedicating one full hour every quarter to discussing some of the topics that are generally taboo and rarely discussed in such close family settings. Here are a few taboo topics that must be discussed:

- *Sex*
- *Money*
- *Death*

So one hour every month adds up to twelve hours a year, and since this is a thirteen hour formula, we still have one extra hour left, which will be used in the next step.

Happy Family Formula Rituals Exercise Download

## Step #2

Every member of the family will use the thirteenth hour individually on his/her birthday. To decide what to discuss during the one-hour window on your birthday, write down all six pillars of the life management system: Health, Wealth, Family, Career/Business, Social Life, and Spirituality. Determine the weakest pillar as well as the best-performing pillar. You may want to use a grading system, like giving each pillar a certain number of points out of ten. Compare your individual pillar scores.

Based on your grades, find the worst-performing pillar and write an action plan to immediately implement ways to improve the pillar's performance. For instance, you might feel that health is your worst pillar, and to improve that, you might want to join a gym, get more sleep, improve the quality of your food, or stop or reduce how much you smoke or consume alcohol. Start following the plan in a very disciplined way.

Now look at the best-performing pillar and go one step further—figure out the reason why this pillar is the best and try to maintain those responsible habits or practices, otherwise this pillar might slip and become the worst pillar. Based on your time and resources, try to balance the four other pillars as well. By following this practice, in a matter of six months or so you will find that all six pillars are quite balanced, and you will end up living a happy and fulfilled life.

Based on those monthly meetings, plan your annual vacations, celebrations, parties, and other relevant activities and put them on the calendar. One of the best practices you can walk away with is to never live a single day without a family vacation booked on your calendar.

**Book Recommendation:** The Abundance Project by Derek Rydall

**Resource Guide:**
https://www.coachrakesh.com/WorkBookLMS

# Chapter 4

# Career/Business

*"Find out what you like doing best and get someone to pay you for doing it." ~**Katharine Whitehorn***

Gone are the days when people used to retire from one job, there was job security, and there was no need to upgrade your skills, just your college/university education was enough to secure your lifelong career. The Internet and the social media age have created a very different world requiring continuous skill upgrades and lifelong learning, which have become the norm for just about every chosen career/business.

When digital cameras came into use, companies like Kodak did not take them seriously and did not adapt to the change, which impacted them in a big way. Similarly, Blockbuster did not take Netflix seriously and lost business. We all know how Uber and Airbnb disrupted the taxi and hotel industries respectively.

We are living in a time of disruption, so the only way to survive and succeed in our career/business is to adopt changes in a timely manner. For that, we have to improve ourselves to stay ahead of changes in the marketplace. The future belongs to artificial intelligence, robotics, and virtual reality. Every new technology or software development

40

creates less and less of a need for humans, so in another decade, outsourcing and automation will disrupt the job market beyond our imagination.

So what is the solution to making our career recession-proof? Without a doubt, we have to continually upgrade our skill set. On top of that, we have to be prepared to shift among different industries and at times, even relocate to new geographical areas. There was a time when experience had value, and earnings were based on the number of years' experience in that particular skill, but today many tools and technologies are being developed that may eliminate the need for previous experience. In addition, younger generations are considered much more productive than the older population.

Just being an employee is no longer the safe way to make your career recession-proof; rather, you must become an entrepreneur on a part-time basis to start, and then switch completely from employee to full-fledged entrepreneur. The new-age entrepreneurs and online marketers and influencers like Gary Vaynerchuk, John Lee Dumas, Pat Flynn, Frank Kern, and Amy Porterfield often suggest that to create a million-dollar sales company, you do not need to fire any employees. Instead, hire contractors from online service providers like www.fiverr.com, www.upwork.com, and many other available online outsourcing platforms.

No matter what industry you're in, you cannot afford not to be online today. For career seekers, a LinkedIn profile is your resume, and your personal website is your business card. Facebook, YouTube, Instagram, and LinkedIn have

41

equipped us with many ways to promote products and services and offer them to the marketplace. For instance, for career seekers, LinkedIn is more than enough help you remain in your desired career, as long as you stay connected with the right people and keep sharing your values on the platform. All the gatekeepers are gone today, so you can communicate directly with the decision-makers to globally showcase your skills and talents to anyone. Some companies allow you to work remotely from the comfort of your home and on your own time schedule.

Current contemporary thought leaders and influencers like Tim Ferriss, who wrote a revolutionary book titled *The 4-Hour Workweek*, have created a wave among the younger generations to leave the 9-to-5 corporate world and design their lifestyle based on their own terms and conditions—no need to conform to the decades-old norms. Another influencer with whom I resonate the most is Gary Vaynerchuk, who has changed the mindset of every generation and provided them with many options to live the life of their own choosing. No need to stick to one job or one profession, just have fun and enjoy your freedom by using lots of easy options to create income as well as an impact that builds your own legacy at the same time.

The only skill you need to build is that of becoming a problem solver. So just identify a problem in the marketplace and provide the solution, and you can get paid for this. The Internet, social media, and technologies have made it easy and affordable to reach out to a global audience and offer your services to them. Today, out of 7.5 billion people globally, more than 5 billion people are

42

connected online, and they are within your reach to serve with your products and services. For instance, identify a problem in the marketplace, provide the solution, and charge $100 per client. Book 100 clients per month and you have 100 X 100 = $10,000 monthly income—this is not at all difficult to do.

In fact, services like the Amazon Affiliate program provide you with a platform where you can set up your associate account without needing to have your own product. Instead, just use their affiliate link to earn a referral commission, which can easily replace today's average salary. The best part is that you can do this from the comfort of your couch using your Smartphone, you don't even need a laptop, only your Smartphone, an Internet connection, and a bank account to receive payments, and you are an entrepreneur.

For experienced people, you can digitize your knowledge and experience in the form of online courses, audio programs, video programs, eBooks, print books and many other ways. The best part of creating a digital product is that you only need to create it once, then you can sell it over and over again. There's no need to stock any inventory and there's no major maintenance. The only skill you need today is a child-like curiosity, creativity, and an abundance mindset, and sky is the limit for you. Online education is turning out to be the biggest revenue-generating resource today. It's a digital economy era, and anyone can utilize the power of the digital revolution to make their career recession-proof.

43

To stand out in the marketplace, we have to equip ourselves with the right skills, mindset, and tools, which will be difficult to master but will give you the most return. One of my virtual mentors, Jim Rohn, said that we should spend five to ten percent of our net income on our personal growth.

Here are a few of the areas in which we need to become an expert and participate in on a regular basis, which will help us stand out:

- **Public speaking**
- **Presentation skills**
- **Webinars**
- **Podcasting**
- **Video content**
- **Social media**
- **Regular valuable content creation and sharing**
- **Attend conferences regularly**
- **Network with influencers**
- **Hire coaches and mentors**
- **Regular skills upgrades**
- **Become an author**

We often try to copy someone else's business/career model without realizing that it may not be the right choice in the long run. The key element is that before starting any venture, we have to find out what our "Zone of Genius" is— some may call it an unfair advantage. This means that we are experts in our particular skill and it comes easily to us, so we will enjoy practicing it. So make sure that your Zone of Genius (ZOG) is being used in your career/business, and that way, even if you face some ups and downs, you will not be disheartened easily. You will be able to keep working at it while enjoying the ride with full passion and enthusiasm.

Another point here is that you need to be really careful before hiring a coach or mentor and make sure that the coach is well aware of your ZOG. Your coach should be sure that your personal ZOG is being used to create your products and services to generate income.

All of sudden coaching and speaking have become quite popular ways of creating a lucrative career. Coaching, mentoring, and consulting can be easily developed to deliver your services for a great fee, and you can deliver these services from the comfort of your own location by utilizing online video conferencing tools like Skype and Zoom.

Many of us get caught up in confusion over technology, making us fearful that it isn't so easy to start our own business, but it doesn't have to be that way. Just focus on your strong skills and hire others who can make up for your weaknesses. If early in your business you think you cannot afford to hire people who have strong skills where yours are weak, then you can learn those skills, as all of these skills are learnable with little effort. Here are the three strategies that can help you launch your lucrative business:

1- **Delegation**
2- **Automation**
3- **Outsourcing**

Nothing can stop you from achieving your desired and realistic goal. Chances are that whatever you are trying to achieve has already been done by someone else, and they have probably created a course, written a book, or some sort of digital product already exists that can provide you step-by-step instructions to recreate the same success. Here is the simple five-step process you can use to achieve any goal you desire:

1. **What do you want**

2. **Why do you want it**

3. **Who has already done it? Reach out to that person for guidance or take his/her courses**

4. **Follow the practices that the person in step 3 followed**

5. **Find an accountability partner to whom you can be accountable to get your desired results by making sure that you execute the necessary steps**

Some people experience imposter syndrome, where they never feel they are ready to create products or services to sell. Often they get caught in a loop, thinking that they need to learn more new skills, which makes them buy one course after another and attend one conference after another, never feeling confident enough to launch their business.

46

The solution for this syndrome is to follow the just-in-time learning concept, which means that you start creating the product and learn only those skills that are needed to move to the next step. Soon you will see your productivity going through the roof, and you'll feel so confident and on top of things that you'll start delivering your products and services to end users much faster. The result is that cash will start flowing into your bank account.

With respect to delivering your finished product, I would like to share a belief of one of the top marketers and thought leaders of our time—the great Seth Godin, who says that if you wait for perfection, it'll be too late. In fact, someone else said that perfection is boring.

**Book Recommendation**: **The 4-Hour Workweek** by *Tim Ferriss*

**Resource Guide***:*
*https://www.coachrakesh.com/WorkBookLMS*

# Chapter 5

# **Social Life**

*"You're the average of the five people you spend the most time with." ~**Jim Rᴐhn***

As a child growing up in India, which I discussed earlier in this book, I never fit into society and hated conformity like hell. I never had the courage to speak up; I always doubted myself and thought that something must have been wrong with me. But everything changed that day I saw the airplane while working with laborers in the rice field—I knew one day I would board a sky machine. That desire brought me from my village to a city called Allahabad (now Prayagraj) where I finished my engineering studies. I moved to New Delhi and started working there, and soon I realized that I might not be able to use my creativity and freedom if I continued working in India.

One day while visiting the American Library in New Delhi with my Keralite friend Jacob, I stumbled upon a book called *The Magic of Thinking Big*. After reading it, I learned one very timely lesson: early in your career, never focus on saving money, but rather focus on finding more streams of income. However, never compromise your lifestyle, because if you are not into drugs, alcohol, gambling, womanizing, or any other bad habits, then by saving

48

money, you will end up compromising your living situation, which will result in living a mediocre and possibly a poor lifestyle.

Basically you would be compromising your poor/mediocre life by not having quality food, clothes, travel, and transportation, and that mindset forced me into expensive living. Soon I realized that my meager earnings in India would not be enough to sustain me, which brought me to the Middle East, where I worked in Bahrain for almost four years as a sales and service engineer. I took care of my immediate family's financial responsibilities like building a house, paying for my sister's wedding, and supporting my siblings.

I made up my mind that I would never settle down back in India, and the Middle East had no option for me to become a permanent resident, so I started looking for alternative options. It was the year 2000, a time when most of the Indian youth were heading to the USA to take advantage of the IT boom during Y2K. I resigned and went to Bangalore, where I completed my Main Frame course. I then left for San Francisco, California in the USA.

But before leaving Bahrain, I applied for Canadian PR (permanent residency). After spending some time in America, one fine day out of curiosity, I called my Uncle Mehta in Delhi, where I used to rent his place. To my surprise, he told me that there was a letter for me from the Canadian consulate to attend an interview for migrating to Canada. I went to the interview, got my Canadian immigration approval, and finally on March 21, 1999, I

49

landed in this beautiful country of Canada and settled here.

I got into the IT industry, married, and became a father when my first son was born, but somehow life felt very stagnant and unsatisfying. Then one day I heard a quote from Jim Rohn: "You're the average of the five people you spend the most time with." I soon realized that my average was very poor. I found a site called www.canada411.com and searched it, gathering a list of people to call. I called 252 families, met thirty-six of them one-on-one, and finally invited fourteen families to my house after shortlisting them based on fifteen selection criteria, including things like age, profession, marital status, and number of kids. These fourteen families became my close social associates, and life started moving along well. We started holding traditional celebrations and vacationing together in groups, both locally and internationally. We also created business-like meetings using the mastermind concept and started sharing our wins, challenges, and commitments, finding accountability partners among the group members, both for males and females.

As a result, many of my new associates switched jobs for better prospects, and a few even shifted from employee to self-employed, finally becoming entrepreneurs. In most cases I was the one who lit the fire under them, and the best part was that this group became a kind of testing ground for me. Since many of my teachings had already worked with individual group members in their careers and businesses, giving them really good results, it gave me the confidence to try a new venture, and I decided to become a life coach as well as a keynote speaker.

I still had difficulty speaking on stage, but my curiosity was piqued one day while doing IT consulting at the Ministry of Transportation here in Toronto. I saw a Toastmasters advertisement that said "We build leaders", and I just walked in as a guest, delivered my first ever Table Topics speech, and won the best TT speaker award.

After that there was no looking back. I became very comfortable on stage. Later on I hired my speaking coach, Steve Lowell (www.SteveLowell.com), for a year, and as part of the course curriculum, I competed among ten speakers at High Impact Speaking, Ottawa and won the most heartfelt speaker award. That day marked the very first time I realized that I had become a mainstream Canadian speaker, and anything was possible for me.

So basically, you should control and design the kind of social circle you want—it should be a positive and complementary circle of people who share common interests and ambitions, which will help you achieve your desired life and career. Having positive and creative families around helps us to build even better bonds among families, and as a result, we can develop more advantageous social networks.

We often take our career or business very seriously, but we frequently ignore our social responsibilities. By the time we realize the kind of damage we have caused to our social values, it's too late to repair. The solution is to look at our social life as a project with continuous efforts for improvement.

Often we have seen—particularly in North America—that we live in big homes but prefer cottage life with friends and family around us. We even feel more adventurous and relaxed when we go camping, which shows that we do not need lots of materialistic possessions to live a motivated and happy life. We feel the most freedom and are more worry-free when we are out in nature and with friends, and both are generally free. We just need the desire to reach out to them with open arms.

Society is a mixture of many different faiths and beliefs, which we refer to as religions as well. Many times we are only aware of our own faith and ignore the teachings and contributions of other faiths in our existence. As a result, we feel and see a lot of friction in our societies, and it need not be that way.

I would like to share something that helped me build my own mindset of love and respect for every faith in our society, hating none. As a result I have close friends from almost every walk of life, and I live with the mindset of the Hindi saying "Basudhaive Kutumbakam", which means that the whole Earth is like one single family.

It's actually the story of my own life experience as to how I developed a "love everyone" attitude. Growing up in my village in India, whenever we kids would get sick, my parents would take us to the Muslim shrine with the faith that we would be cured by the blessings of the shrine.

As an adult, I went to Delhi and started working, but as the eldest sibling I was playing the role of a father in terms of responsibility, especially since I was from a poor family. I needed to earn a lot of money, which I was not able to do at first, so I thought that going to the Middle East would be a better option.

Then a Sikh gentleman, Mr. N. P. Singh, helped me get a job in Bahrain, where I worked for about four years as a sales and service engineer. Sometime later, a Jain gentleman, Mr. Rakesh Jain, planted a seed in me to switch my career focus from hardware to software. As a result, I decided to resign and go to Bangalore to do some additional coursework, and I finally went to the USA as an IT professional.

But before leaving Bangalore, a Christian gentleman, Mr. Joe Martin, helped me prepare my immigration application for Canada. After staying for a while in the USA, my Canadian immigration application was approved. When I joined Toastmasters to improve my speaking skills, I met a Jewish gentleman, Earl Tucker, who became my mentor and helped me become comfortable with public speaking. That opened up a new possibility, awakening my desire to become a public speaker.

Adding everything all together, I was born a Hindu, a Muslim shrine cured my sickness, a Sikh gentleman guided me to a better earning opportunity in the Middle East, a Jain gentleman advised me about getting a new career in Information Technology, a Christian gentleman helped me migrate to Canada, and finally a Jewish gentleman mentored me, or rather gave me the voice to live my public speaking dream. Considering all these helpful influences in my life, how can I hate any faith or person when those diverse social experiences gave me my loving mindset and taught me to treat the whole Earth as one big family? Since that time, I have engaged in some relatively unusual practices, which I do without fail—one of them that I do regularly is to meet one stranger every day, with the goal of leaving that person with a smile on their face.

Sometimes I just stand behind an elderly person in the grocery line and pay for a few items that she/he cannot easily afford because they lack enough money. I do many other favors for people in our society without paying attention to their sex, race, age, color, or faith because they all have contributed to my success directly or indirectly, and it's now my turn to repay them.

Social media and the Internet have made our social life so interesting and meaningful—it's even possible for anyone to make his/her living just by utilizing the power of social media and the Internet. Today the entry cost to the business world is zero.

## 13 Family Friends Group-Building Process to Transform Your Social Life

There was a time when we lived our entire lives with the same set of friends, as there weren't as many options to meet new people. But today social media has made our reach so broad that we have many options from which to choose our friends. Here I am going to use Jim Rohn's quote, "You're the average of the five people you spend the

54

most time with" as a basis to design a thirteen family friends group to help you have a successful social life.

In keeping with the title of this book, *6 Pillars of the Life Management System,* we are going to use six pillars as the main criteria to find appropriate friends. Here are the following six steps you can take to find those additional twelve families so that, including you, there will be a group of thirteen families in your family friends group:

1. **Create ten or more no-compromise conditions to choose your family friends**

2. **Now find six families that are stronger in each of the six pillars than your family**

3. **Find six more families who are really poor or weaker than your family in one of these pillars**

4. **Now including you, there are thirteen families in the group**

5. **Plan out your daily, weekly, monthly, quarterly, and annual agendas**

6. **Create rules and regulations to remove/replace a group member**

With this group set up, you have at least six families who are much better than you in certain pillars and will inspire you to grow. But if everybody is better than you, you and your family members might feel somewhat inferior, or in extreme situations, you may feel depressed. For those times, you have six families who are much weaker or poorer than you who will boost your ego, allowing you to feel better and superior. Enjoy your designed social life instead of living a default and boring one.

**Book Recommendation**: How to Win Friends and Influence People by *Dale Carnegie*

**Resource Guide***:*
*https://www.coachrakesh.com/WorkBookLMS*

# Chapter 6

# Spirituality

*"Live worry-free and leave regret-free."* **~Rakesh Mishra**

Coming from northern India and born in the Hindu religion, at a very early stage of my life, I was exposed to Eastern spiritual practices like yoga and meditation. For some strange reason, I got it into my head that these were religious practices meant to be practiced only by gurus and yogis. In other words, only spiritual gurus are supposed to practice them, they were not for ordinary people like me. In fact, I never practiced or believed in them until I was in my early 40s, and then one day, everything changed.

It was April 2015 and for the very first time, I was attending a personal development and marketing conference in Santa Clara called Experts Academy by Brendon Burchard. It was a three-day event, and on the last day, Brendon said from the stage that he was going to discuss spirituality. I was a little skeptical about what this young white Western guy was going to teach me about spirituality, but at the same time, I was very curious and open to listening to him with full attention and sincerity. In his opening line, he said that he'd read many books, most of which were full of complicated explanations and didn't really teach readers how to practice spirituality. He said that meditation is one of the core practices of spirituality, but these books hardly ever teach that.

Brendon said that he'd met an Indian guru who taught him in a very simple way to customize his own meditation practice. Brendon called it "Release Meditation", and he explained that you spend just twenty minutes of quiet time in a calm place, play pre-recorded music in the background, and say a word with which you associate your sense of spirituality; Brendon uses the word "release". Just say release, release, release using different pitches and pacing. In fact, if you do an online search for Brendon Release Meditation on YouTube, you will find Brendon's video with thirty minutes of pre-recorded guided meditation that you can follow.

After the conference was over, I came back to Toronto. In those days my life was kind of a mess; so many difficulties were making me very restless and not at ease. Every morning I was tired and restless, filled with anxiety and irritability. I just wanted to be on my own and hardly wanted to talk to anybody. I had no idea that I was going through a type of depression.

In the afternoon I would feel exhausted and full of worries. I had so many negative thoughts that my life was hell, that nothing was going to work out, and that I was going to lose my health, job, and relationship. I listened two or three times to Brendon's Release Meditation and thought about giving it a try. In the beginning, I was hardly able to sit more than five minutes—my mind was rushing with even more thoughts than normal, but I decided to give it a try for a few weeks.

In the first week I sat quietly for five to ten minutes without any stillness of mind, but from the second week on, I sat for the full twenty minutes and followed the instructions given by Brendon. I decided that no matter what, I was going to sit for the full twenty minutes. To my surprise around the fifth week, I started enjoying these meditation sessions. Not only did my sleep quality improve, but in the office I felt less and less tired, and slowly those negative thoughts started being replaced by happy thoughts. The best part was that I started enjoying talking to my wife, children, and friends again.

My blood pressure reading became totally normal and even went below normal. Thanks to Brendon's free Release Meditation videos, my life was changed forever, and now I never miss my meditation sessions no matter where I am. Sometimes I even do them on a plane or in my office chair. For me, spirituality is now simple, and Release Meditation is the tool I use to practice my spirituality, which makes my mind calm.

After practicing meditation for a few years, meditation has now become my path to spirituality. Basically, meditation is nothing but reaching a completely blank state of mind. Once I gained full control of my mind, I slowly started reading some more books and articles and watching many videos. Around 2016, I encountered one more gem of a person named Hal Elrod, who released a book titled *The Miracle Morning*. When he visited Toronto, I met him at a "Socialite " event and bought his book. I read it and simply loved it.

59

I then combined Release Meditation and *The Miracle Morning*'s morning practices to customize my morning power hours. That put my life securely on the Spirituality Highway, and I began enjoying every minute of my existence. The result is that since the beginning of the year 2018, I became a mindset coach and motivational speaker, sharing my stories and helping many people transform their lives. This book is the result of all the practices that transformed my life, giving me motivation, significance, and purpose.

As I mentioned at the beginning, when I was in Cuba, I discovered that my life's purpose was to reach out and help a billion people globally in some positive way before my last breath, but I was not sure how to help them, as I was struggling with my own life. However, Release Meditation and *The Miracle Morning* practices have helped me transform my life and understand people's situations better so I can help them. Now I am helping lots of couples, individuals, and corporate groups, teaching them how to achieve balance in their life's six pillars and live a fully motivated, inspired life according to their own personal purpose.

The core of spirituality is to live with mindfulness, which comes when your mind stays calm and you are living your life's purpose with full passion. But for many people, it's difficult to find what their purpose is—believe it or not, it's actually not very difficult. You just need to reflect on your life on a regular basis by sitting quietly for fifteen minutes every week and contemplating on your current and past life. Think about what you have enjoyed doing, and slowly you will find the purpose of your life, as this reflection session will give you the necessary pointers and clues. In my case, I reflected for a week in Cuba and wrote 1,700 pages, and when I started reading those pages, I came to realize that I am happiest when I help people around me reach their potential and live it. So just sitting quietly and thinking is the best way to find your purpose.

In addition to meditation, here are some more practices we can use to involve spirituality in our day-to-day lives:

- *Learn and practice philosophies from all walks of life*
- *Learn and practice detachment, especially from the materialistic world*
- *Get into the habit of reading great books*
- *Learn and practice enjoying your own company*
- *Meet and interact with strangers. I meet one stranger daily and leave them with a smile*
- *Visit and explore new places*
- *Spend time alone with nature*
- *Document your journey*
- *Do not expect anything from anybody*
- *Do not make any assumptions that lead to negativity in your mind*
- *Do not take things personally*
- *Think and reflect regularly*
- *Declutter physical space*
- *Declutter mental space*
- *Procrastinate your worries*
- *Avoid comparisons*

- *Focus on your strongest skills*
- *Surround yourself with those who lift up your spirit*
- *Develop an attitude to accept and face the worse*
- *Develop empathy for others*
- *Accept that you came into this world alone, you will go out alone, and everybody dies someday*
- *Accept that like a movie, each of us is playing our role, and life is like a film*
- *Learn to live in a day-tight compartment. Anybody can live happily for just today, and if every day of your life is just about today, you will end up living a happy and satisfied life*
- *Happiness is a hobby and can be developed easily like other hobbies*
- *Being happy is a choice*
- *Develop a mental toughness shield around yourself that is so strong, negative thoughts will not disturb your peace of mind*
- *Instead of simulating our worst-case scenarios that have not happened yet, we can train ourselves to deal with them only if they actually occur*
- *The mind doesn't understand the difference between real and imaginary*
- *Learn to develop childlike curiosity about the things around us*
- *Engage in learning something new regularly*
- *Regularly ask WHY and review your passions and interests*
- *Regularly try to live without the objects and*

*relationships you feel it's impossible to live without*
- *Do fast regularly or live just for a day on only fluid food or water*

Why has spirituality suddenly become a global phenomenon?

Lately people have lost their peace of mind, and they're suddenly realizing that material possessions are not a source of permanent happiness. So they've started seeking alternative options, and spirituality gives them a solution up to a certain point. Basically after a certain age and life experience, we start looking to transform our lives so that we can live a purposeful life, and the only core purpose of life is to stay HAPPY, or in other words, "live worry-free and leave regret-free". Your life transformation stage depends on how you manage your life's six pillars. You will fall into one of the following three stages of life transformation:

- **Survival**
- **Success**
- **Significance**

The majority of us are just surviving and living in poverty or in mediocrity. The definition of success is subjective, but still, a very small percentage of people are living successful lives, and most third world countries are still living in survival mode. When you are living in "survival" or "success" mode, basically you are living for yourself or for your close family.

63

But the "significance" transformation happens when, with your presence on this planet or with your products and services, you help others improve their lives or fulfill their purpose in life. Then you can say that you have transformed your life stage to significance, and that's the ultimate type of spiritual living we are all seeking on this planet.

In other words, real happiness or fulfillment in life comes when we start living for others. That's what Nelson Mandela, Mother Teresa, Martin Luther King, and Gandhi did, as well as many more spiritual souls who devoted their lives to the service of others.

The great speaker Zig Ziglar so beautifully said that whatever you want in your life, you will get, if you just help enough people achieve what they want in their lives. He is saying the same thing, but he was probably more inclined toward a materialistic context.

One thing is very clear here—our thoughts are the main drivers for our feelings, which are directly responsible for our mental peace. Here I would like to summarize the model of one of my virtual coaches, Brooke Castillo, who created the CTFAR model:

- **Circumstances**
- **Thoughts**
- **Feelings**
- **Actions**
- **Results**

64

This simply means that our circumstances trigger our thoughts, our thoughts trigger our feelings, our feelings trigger our actions, and our actions decide our results. So no matter what your mind is thinking right now, you can backtrack your thoughts in order to drill down to the circumstances where those thoughts originated.

These circumstances further fall into two categories: (1) we can do something about them, or (2) we cannot do anything about them. So just focus and reflect on those areas where you can do something about them, and that will help you control your thoughts so that you can finally improve the end results, which are responsible for your peace and happiness in general. This model can be used as a tool to enhance your spiritual living.

One final way to improve your spiritual living is to have control over your negative thoughts that accumulate over time from our unpleasant relationships. The following four practices can help you declutter your mind, which is full of those negative thoughts that have eaten away at your peace.

## Say Sorry

Often people stop talking in relationships, and the other person thinks it was not their fault; they think it was yours. In fact, it was not your fault, but that situation often bothers you and makes you uncomfortable in social situations where you will encounter that person, and you have to avoid that interaction.

65

The best solution is to make a list of such people and simply call, write, text, or meet with them, or create an audio or video message and say you're sorry. That's it.

Remember, even if you are not at fault, you are doing it for your own sake and peace of mind. Of course, you have to be careful when not to say you're sorry because it might put you in a very awkward situation or get you into legal trouble, so just consider the situation and deal with it accordingly.

But most often these are simple issues that steal your peace of mind due to miscommunications and misunderstandings, so it's better to resolve them as quickly as possible. Then keep your distance from such people or at least be careful in your dealings with them. And of course, if it was your fault, then by all means, go ahead and say you're sorry and live with abundant happiness and peace.

## Forgive Them

In many cases, you know that these people are very aware that the situation was their fault, but their ego won't allow them to take the initiative to apologize or resolve the conflict. In that case, use the most suitable form of communication to reach out to them and forgive them. It might be possible that a person still will not want to be on speaking terms with you, and that's fine. At least you've been clear, and you will have achieved peace within yourself. Just remember that you did this for your own peace of mind.

## Forgive Yourself

In many cases you know that something was your fault. In that case, simply reach out to the party concerned using the appropriate means of communication and say you're sorry. In same rare cases, either the person is no longer living or is not in a position to be reached and it is impossible to communicate with them. In such a situation, we tend to live with guilt and are not able to forgive ourselves. In those times, remind yourself that we are all human beings and not superheroes, so we can make mistakes. Then just forgive yourself. While this is happening, it's not always so easy, but we have to analyze the situation in addition to our possible options, then take action accordingly. Often forgiving ourselves for something that is our own fault is the best approach.

## Say Thanks

In our busy lives, often we don't pay attention to the fact that many of our close friends, relatives, or family members have supported us in difficult times, and we hardly ever remember to say a simple thanks. Other parties involved may hold a grudge, as they are expecting a kind "thank you" at least or some type of acknowledgement. Based on the seriousness of the situation, convey your thanks if possible. You can meet with them, write to them, or if it's not too expensive, meet for coffee or lunch or dinner and convey your thanks with full sincerity.

Spirituality becomes a must as you age, but it can be practiced at any age. With that, I hope I was able to help you manage your six pillars of life to live a more fulfilled and happy life. Good Luck.

**Book Recommendation**: **The Power of Now** by *Eckhart Tolle*

**Resource Guide**:
*https://www.CoachRakesh.com/WorkBookLMS*

# Chapter 7

# Beyond – Next Steps

Now, what's **NEXT**...

In the last six chapters I shared my journey and discussed how it helped me shape my career, giving me the ideas and motivation to move beyond on my stuck feelings. I found that knowingly or unknowingly, I was just after these two words that showed me a clear path: "stretch" and "act". Here I want to walk through once again the stretch and act phases of my life journey so far, which are summed up in the following seven major stretches.

## Stretch #1

At the early age of seven, I learned from my aunt who was rich and lived in Dubai and the USA that to become rich, I would have to leave India—living in my village was not an option. So one day I decided to take my very first "stretch", and at the age of seventeen I left my village and went to the city of Allahabad (now Prayagraj). I supported myself and paid for my education by teaching the kids of rich people. I finished my engineering studies and was ready to enter the next phase of my life—searching for a job, since I did not get selected for any job through campus interviews.

## Stretch #2

During my last year of college, as part of the college tour I went to New Delhi, where I spent almost a week. I realized that if I was going to become something big, I would have to move to a place like New Delhi. I would be stretching every day to adapt to the fast-paced and challenging lifestyle, but for some strange reason, a silent seed got planted in me to live in this magical city, which would open the door to some big possibilities for me.

Another reason I knew I needed to move there was that since I did not get any jobs from my campus interviews, I had very few options—I could either apply for a government job without any certainty as to whether I'd get one or join some small private company just to survive. But New Delhi came into my mind again and again as I started developing a love for that city, and one day I took my second major "stretch" and boarded the Prayagraj Express train from Allahabad to New Delhi.

## Stretch #3

On September 23, 1991, I reached New Delhi with my classmate Vivek Savita, who knew one of his schoolmates could help us find a place to rent. In a few weeks, I got a job in an electronics company that manufactured Uninterrupted Power Supplies, but in just a few months I became bored because every day for eight whole hours, I had to sit, stare at, and test Printed Circuit Boards. So I started looking for a better job and got a position in another company as a service engineer. It was much better, as part of my job was to visit client locations and meet different people, and I loved having conversations with them. During this time I was introduced to a book titled *The Magic of Thinking Big* by David J. Schwartz. One thing I learned from this book is to never focus on saving money in the early stage of your career. Instead, focus on finding more streams of income, because if you do not have any bad habits like gambling, drugs, alcohol, or womanizing, you will be saving money that could instead benefit you and your family. You will become addicted to mediocre living and soon will surrender to your circumstances and die poor.

My lifestyle in India was very expensive and my earnings were not able to support my lifestyle. It was time for my third "stretch", and I applied for my passport and started looking for opportunities in the Middle East by asking every person possible for information. To my surprise, in a matter of only six months, I got an offer from a company in Bahrain, and a few months later, I was working in Bahrain as a sales and service engineer.

After spending three years in Bahrain, I was earning good money and was able to meet my immediate financial responsibility for my family, like building a house, financing my sister's wedding, and paying my brother's tuition fee. I now started feeling a little restless as I was over twenty-seven years old and about to get married. However, the thought always frightened me to just get married, have kids, raise them, grow old, and die. Slowly I developed a fascination with moving out to the Western world for a better lifestyle, but I had no clue how to move forward.

Once again my "power of asking" came to my rescue, and it was time for my next "stretch".

## Stretch #4

One day one of my new friends, Rakesh Jain, who used to work at Yateem Air Conditioning, advised me to try going to the USA as an IT professional, but I had no clue about IT and had not done any programming. He insisted that there was expected to be a phenomenon called Y2K (a potential issue with computer systems being unable to switch to the year 2000) and I just needed to take a thirty-day course in India to get an H-1B work visa to the USA. I was ready for my fourth "stretch", so I resigned from my job in Bahrain and went to Bangalore (now Bengaluru) and registered for a month-long mainframe course. I landed in San Francisco, California on October 10, 1998.

After spending some time in America, my Canadian immigration application was approved, and I moved to Canada. I got a job and after few years, got married and had my first son. Life started moving but soon became a little stagnant, and I got a bit restless; it was once again time to "stretch". When I went to Cuba alone to find the purpose of my life, after spending one week writing 1,700 pages, I read those pages reflecting on my life and realized that I feel the happiest when I'm helping and mentoring people to find their true potential. It was then that I decided to become a billionaire—to reach out and help a billion people before my last breath. I went back to Toronto with that plan in mind, and I was ready once again for my next "stretch".

## Stretch #5

All excited about reaching and helping a billion people, I first needed to help my family, and I made a plan that over the next ten years, I would make enough money to retire financially on my forty-fifth birthday. Then I could help people full-time, but first I needed to save roughly $2.5 million—the question was *how*? Once again my powerful tool of asking came to my rescue, and after asking friends and colleagues and researching on Google, YouTube, and Workopolis, I realized that it was time to leave my full-time job and go into consulting. Once I did that, my earnings increased by almost three times as much as I had been making, but it was still not enough to save $250,000 annually in order to fulfill my $2.5 million target in the next ten years.

Again, after utilizing the power of asking, I decided to go for my next "stretch" and started placing people in jobs as a recruiter in addition to my consulting work, and every placement fetched me an additional $4,000 to $5,000. I was now in much better financial condition. The time came when I had almost $200,000 in the bank, but I didn't know what to do with the money. One day while listening to Randhir Chahal's radio program, I found out about real estate investing and that the most important thing was location, location, location. In those days I used to live in Scarborough, Ontario in a semi-detached 1,700 sq. ft. house, but it was time for my next major "stretch" to play BIG.

## Stretch #6

Over the long Canada Day weekend, I sat in front of my computer and made a few calls to my real estate agent and friends, and again my best tool—the power of asking—came to my rescue. I discovered that Richmond Hill, Oakville, and Bridal Path were the best locations to buy real estate.

I drove my Honda Accord to Richmond Hill and parked in front of a house with an "Open House" sign, but I had no idea what it meant. So I went inside and toured the house; I loved this 3,500 sq. ft. house with its walkout basement and beautiful stretch of ravine trail. To cut a long story short, I bought this magnificent dream house the same night, and I've been living there since 2006.

At that point I started teaching all these experiences and lessons I learned from my stretches to my family, friends, their friends, and work colleagues for free. Slowly I realized that what I was doing is called coaching. Through word of mouth, I started becoming known as a success story, so I started exploring social media and attending conferences, and the seed was planted to become a coach.

But something was missing—I didn't know what it was, so again I started asking and observing other coaches. I found out that the missing piece was public speaking, which I needed to master. One day I joined Toastmasters, which changed my life forever. Later on I started speaking to a wide variety of groups like Momondays, Rotary Clubs, Lions Clubs, and many other well-known associations. I had reached the point financially where I could say that money is not everything, and it was time to go for my final "stretch".

## Stretch #7

Now I had a few paid coaching clients and I started speaking at every possible opportunity, which I enjoyed, but I always had that feeling that it wasn't enough. I had a negative internal dialogue that said, *Rakesh, you are a brown-skinned guy, and this coaching and speaking industry is mostly a white-dominated market, so you will not be accepted into the mainstream.* But once again I used my favorite tool, the power of asking, and decided to hire my very first paid speaking coach, Steve Lowell, for one year. I started learning the craft, and then the day came when I had to compete among ten speakers at High Impact Speaking, Ottawa. Out of ten speakers, eight were white speakers, and I won the Most Heartfelt Speaker award.

On that day, my worry about not being accepted into the mainstream was eliminated, and I developed a lion's confidence. I was ready for my seventh "stretch"—quitting my IT consulting and going full-time with coaching and speaking. March 31, 2017 was my last day of consulting for the Ministry of Transportation, and I began living my life's mission of reaching and helping a billion people before my last breath; I often give my speech titled "Meet The Real Slumdog Billionaire".

So my curiosity tool, the power of asking, always came to my rescue and helped me, giving me my next "stretch" beyond my comfort zone to find my next calling so I could ACT on it to live life to my full potential and purpose.

So...

- **What is your curiosity tool?**
- **What is your next stretch?**
- **What is your next act?**

It's all about staying curious, creative, and passionate about our circumstances. Anything is possible if we really observe and focus on our surroundings, which will always give us a clue as to what we like the most, which is what really put me in my flow state. Soon you will able to identify your true calling, and then every day will be like a vacation. Then money becomes part of it and starts coming to you in abundance automatically.

I always recommend the following exercise to my clients, which I learned on my Cuba trip. It often delivers results and is worth trying, since you won't lose anything; rather, it will help you know yourself better.

Just before starting the exercise, set an intention in your mind that you are going to find out some amazing things about yourself, such as your secrets, your interests, your ZOG, your strengths, your flow conditions, your untapped limitless potential, your pending you. In general you will be introducing to yourself who you are and finding out what you are hungry for and what will make you complete!

## "Beyond You" Exercise

## What you need

- Pad of paper
- Pen or pencil
- Soothing music of your choice
- Reading glasses if you need them
- A glass or bottle of water
- You may want to wear a light spray of your favorite perfume
- Dress in very loose casual and comfortable clothing
- Go where you will not be disturbed for the next three to four hours

## How to prepare yourself

- For individuals who drink alcohol, just drink lightly, like a glass of wine
- For individuals who don't drink alcohol, have a glass of juice or lemon water
- Avoid sodas unless they're your favorite and help you relax
- Use the washroom
- Let family members know that you are not available for the next three to four hours
- Sit down and do five to ten minutes of meditation
- If you've never meditated, just sit quietly for five to ten minutes and enjoy the music

## How to do self-exploration

It's time to pick up your pen or pencil and start recording YOU on the pad.

- Now start with your youngest memories and continue through to the current moment, recording your whole life in terms of events, which are going to be like scenes in a movie

- Write about major events like your youngest memory, your first day at school, etc

- You should have at least four events for every year you've spent on this planet starting from the first year you remember

- Now start expanding on each of these events as much as you can

- One of the reasons behind this exercise is to identify the patterns of what you really liked

- Another reason behind this exercise is to find your fears and limitations

- It might take more than one sitting to recall your entire life journey

- You may want to write only the headlines of each event in the first sitting and then details in subsequent sittings

- These events are like scenes in movies, and the details are like screenplays

78

- Once you finish this whole exercise, you may want to edit and reorganize your details, removing any redundant content

- Now you are ready to go really deep into it by reading this autobiography of yours like a separate person and see which traits of the protagonist (in this case, you) you really like, and make a note of them

- After completing the above step, you will be able to find your real likes, your ZOG, flow patterns, etc. Now it's time to act on those areas and choose the career/business where those newly found traits or interests can be utilized

- You may want to publish this "book of you" or you may want to hire someone as a ghostwriter to write it for you. You also may want to develop speeches from this content

Once you finish this exercise, you are going to be a different person. Most of my clients find the meaning and purpose of their life this way and have new clarity as to what they really want to do. They are no longer living merely for survival or success, but rather they are going beyond and living a life of true significance.

I hope this exercise revealed to you some positive aspects of your life and gave you clarity about what you want to do next. But if you still need some help and mentoring, I would be happy to help you out—just reach out to me at the following email address with the subject line "Beyond Help Requested" and describe one of the major concerns about which you are seeking clarity.

79

Write to me at rakesh@CoachRakesh.com

Or you may want to book a thirty-minutes complimentary discovery call at the link below. If it's not too difficult, be ready with responses for the following two questions:

**Question #1:** If money and time were not issues, what one thing would you like to do for the rest of your life, even if you were not paid for it?

**Question #2:** If you knew that you would not fail, what one thing would you want to start doing right now?

>> Tap here to get more information and to set up your complimentary session today. <<

# Conclusion

The whole idea behind writing this book is to help you make yourself recession-proof, worry-free, and regret-free and live life with purpose, meaning, and happiness.

Here once again is a summary of the lessons from this book that can be used to transform your life, which involves both personal and business goals.

- Do a regular review of all six pillars and create a preventive maintenance plan to keep them in balance

- Implement thirteen-hour family rituals regularly with necessary upgrades

- Meet one stranger daily or modify the meeting frequency based on your level of comfort

- Set goals for each pillar by using the SMART goal-setting formula, and achieve these goals by using the WWWRF formula covered in detail in chapter 2

- Regularly analyze your "why" against all six pillars and continually adjust them accordingly

- Once you turn fifty, try to work mostly on your Significance level rather than on the Survival and Success levels, even if you have to make compromises in some of your other areas of interest

- The above summary will help you live your life simply and enable you to easily avoid complications

81

Feel free to reach out to me if you have any specific questions or concerns.

To connect with Coach Rakesh, go to
https://www.coachrakesh.com/contact.

# Strategy Session Invitation

Are you ready to set up a complimentary strategy session?

Are you ready to learn how you can transform your life and start living with the same energy, enthusiasm, curiosity, happiness, and freedom as a child?

The only question we ask in our no-pitch session is: "Tell me, what bothers you every waking hour of your life?" This is not a sales call. Our only intention is to see if we can help you live your life worry-free and regret–free by finding the purpose of your life, and by helping you find the resources you need to live your purpose and inspire others to do the same.

Due to time constraints, the call must be limited to 30 minutes.

Are you ready to get started?

>> Tap here to get more information and to set up your complimentary session today. <<

# About The Author

Rakesh Mishra began his life as a poor farm boy in a village in India. He grew up in poor conditions with no electricity, no automobiles, no TV, no phone, and no example to show him any other world of possibilities. He grew beyond those conditions anyway and not only changed his life and location but was able to retire by age forty-five so that he could spend the rest of his life helping others.

Rakesh Mishra is an award-winning speaker and mindset coach who has addressed audiences from more than 200 stages and inspired and motivated more than 100,000 people in several countries to have a mission. Dedicated passionately to his own mission, Mishra's vision is to influence the lives of a billion people in his lifetime. The sought-after keynote and breakout speaker promises to present a simple concept to help people develop mental toughness and a recession-proof mindset, which prepares them to deal with their personal and business life with great success.

With a focus on building the right mindset, Mishra offers his Life Management System program that covers the six pillars of life, including Health, Wealth, Family, Career/Business, Social Life, and Spirituality.

"These are the six pillars that affect people in one way or another," says Mishra. "One or more of these pillars is affecting your journey through life. Toward this end, I help people understand their hidden self, explore their deepest desires, and realize their potential. I provide individuals and groups with coaching in self-improvement, clarity, confidence, mental toughness, public speaking, interpersonal skills, and corporate training as well as salesmanship."

The journey has not been an easy one for the coach who calls himself a real "slumdog" and actually became a millionaire, achieving financial freedom on his forty-fifth birthday. He now shares what he learned through speaking,

85

workshops, and seminars and often delivers his speech titled "Meet The Real Slumdog Billionaire".

"I believe that despite numerous challenges, if I can do it, then anyone can change their destiny. The key thing is to explore your internal path and follow that defined path to success," says Mishra.

How did he do it?

In the following award-winning speech, which took twenty-five years to prepare and was delivered at High Impact Speaking, Ottawa, Canada, Coach Rakesh reveals some of his strategies as to how he was able to become financially free at age forty-five. He also shares one of his most challenging moments of life that made him think about taking his own life, but...

>> Tap to watch "Meet The Real Slumdog Billionaire"<<

To connect with Coach Rakesh, go to www.CoachRakesh.com/contact.

# Acknowledgments

My whole life has been inspired and supported by so many people and places, and this is the best opportunity to acknowledge them one by one.

**The three most important women in my life:**

**My Mom**

Who is no longer with us, but she taught me to have clarity in what I wanted and to act with full focus, using whatever resources were available to me without worrying or caring about how to get there.

**My first wife, the late Shilpa Mishra**

Who taught me the importance of relationships and not to give too much importance to the money. She also taught me that life is too short and not to wait for perfect conditions to start something worth pursuing; instead just do it and adjust later.

It seems like she knew she would have a very short life, and that may have been the reason she always used to say that life is too short. She passed away at the young age of thirty-five while delivering our second son, Anuj. She left us, but she gave me a story to share, and that is the reason this book came into existence.

87

## My wife now, Rinke Mishra

Who helped me to overcome the trauma I was going through after losing the two most important women in my Life. She taught me to control my emotions, forget about the past, live in the present moment, not try to make everybody happy, and develop mental toughness. This book would never have been possible without her support, taking care of the whole family both here in Canada and in India so that I could focus on my writing.

## My father

Who always believed in "simple living and high thinking", and that trait of his transferred strongly into me. Another important lesson he taught me that helped a lot is "no work is small work", do everything with full passion, sincerity, and hard work.

## Bollywood

After growing up as a child in poor financial conditions and always searching for ways to become rich, I moved to a city called Allahabad and started teaching in order to support my own studies and survival. At times I wondered why my parents gave birth to me if they could not provide the basic means of living for us. I was always mad at them, but during that same time I started watching Bollywood movies, especially Amitabh Bachchan's movies, and one thing I found in common in all his movies was that he had no family support system and always ended up in a rags-to-riches kind of story.

88

I lived by the saying, "If you have nothing, anything is possible." Basically in my mind I killed my parents and told myself that I was now like an Amitabh Bachchan movie, so I should go and turn myself into something big like him because I had nothing to lose. I started to take all possible chances without worrying about rejection, failure, or defeat. So thanks to Bollywood for giving me hope and the courage to dream.

## Abdul Wahid and the Middle East

Thanks to Mr. Abdul Wahid, who gave me an opportunity to work in Bahrain and Dubai. That opportunity came just at the right time, as I needed a big chunk of money to build a house and finance my sister's wedding and my brother's education. Thanks to Bahrain and Dubai and all the staff of Gulf Market International for providing me support, without which this journey to write this book would never have been possible.

## Six Different Major Global Faiths

### Hindu Faith

Being born Hindu, I would like to acknowledge and thank all the values and traditions that help me serve the world till my last breath. There is a Sanskrit phrase that comes from Hindu teachings, "Vasudhaiva Kutumbakam", which means that planet Earth as a whole is one family, and I literally started following that belief.

## Muslim Faith

During my childhood, whenever we fell sick, our parents used to take us to those Muslim mazars (shrines) with the hope and faith that just touching and praying in them would cure us. So I would like to thank those holy shrines for curing me, otherwise it would never have been possible to carry out this beautiful and inspiring journey of mine.

## Sikh Faith

When I started working in Delhi, and since I was the eldest sibling and son in the family, responsibility-wise I was playing my father's role, and I needed lots of money to support my family, as previously mentioned. A great human named Sardar N. K. Singh helped me connect with a friend of his, Mr. Abdul Wahid from Bahrain, who recruited me as a sales and service engineer and provided me an opportunity to work overseas, which was very badly needed at that time. So thanks to the Sikh gentleman Mr. N. K. Singh for the timely favor and support.

## Jain Faith

When I moved to Bahrain and after working there a few years, I met a true gentleman from the Jain faith, Mr. Piyush Jain, and soon we became friends. By this time I had earned enough money to fulfill my immediate family's financial obligations and was feeling a bit restless as to what to do next. I developed an inclination to move to the Western world, in particular the USA, but I didn't know how.

One day while chatting with Mr. Piyush Jain, he suggested I resign and go to India to take some quick courses in mainframe computer programming. He said I could get an H-1B visa and go to the USA, as there was a high demand for IT professionals in the USA due to the potential Y2K crisis. I did exactly what he advised, and as they say, the rest is history, and soon I was living in San Francisco, California. So thanks to Mr. Piyush Jain for guiding me at just the right time, otherwise it would never have been possible for me to come to one of the richest continents in the world, North America.

## Christian Faith

After I made my decision to go to the USA, one day while still living in Bahrain I saw an advertisement in the *Gulf Daily News* about a Canadian immigration seminar being held at the Sheraton Bahrain, given by a gentleman named Mr. T. Jacob. I attended the seminar and he convinced me that Canada would be the best destination for me in the long run and that it was one of the best places to live on the planet. I followed his advice.

After some time, my Canadian immigration was approved, and I landed in this beautiful country on March 21, 1999, where I've lived for the last twenty years. After living here two decades, I can say that Mr. T Jacob was so right, and thanks to his advice and guidance, and after visiting more than twenty-five percent of the world, I realize that the Canadian passport is one of the most respected and accepted passports in the world.

## Anuj Victor Singh, Seventh-day Adventist Christian

Anuj, one of my oldest friends, whom I met during my transition from the Middle East (Bahrain) to the USA during the Y2K- IT boom days in Bangalore now Bengaluru. We matched intellectually and personally, and I know this friendship is going to continue for a long time. After a brief stay in the USA, I moved to Canada, and Anuj also decided to move to Canada.

We shared an apartment for a long time. Though he has an accounting (ICWA) background, he saw me involved in Oracle DBA and recognized the market demand of DBAs in those days, so he decided to pursue his career with Oracle. His dedication and determination made him an Oracle DBA within the year, and now after almost twenty years, he is still working with Oracle DBA and has his own team of DBAs working for him.

I still remember after I decided to financially retire on March 31, 2017 from the Ministry of Transportation as an IT consultant in order to pursue my long-awaited dream of becoming a motivational speaker and business coach, there was a little insecurity in the back of my mind regarding that huge consulting income that suddenly stopped.

I remember talking to Anuj, who has a big influence today in the IT market with many people working for him as a consultant. He said, "Rakesh, do not worry, just follow your passion, and any time you feel that you want to come back full-time or part-time as a consultant, just give me a call. You can start any day you want, and you can even work from home, or for that matter, anywhere in the world."

92

So he gave me that open offer to work from any location, which was a big morale boost that I needed at that time. In fact, I did work with him as well. So I would like to thank my dear friend Anujj Victor Singh for providing me the unconditional support I needed the most at that time. It probably would never have been possible to make my transition to the speaking and coaching world so smoothly without his support. Thanks, Anuj.

## Jewish Faith

One day during our Downsview Toastmasters weekly meeting, I delivered my speech, and after that meeting was over, one of the senior members of the club, Mr. Jake Ackerman (a Jewish gentleman), mentioned to me that he loved my energy, enthusiasm, and the passion in my delivery. But he did not understand anything I said, as I was talking too fast with overlapping and unclear phrases as well as a heavy Indian accent. He offered to mentor me in speaking skills if I was open to it, which I gladly accepted. And as they say, the rest is history.

So I would like to thank my dear friend and mentor Mr. Jake Ackerman for mentoring me, otherwise I would never have dared to speak from the stage, and all these stories would never have gone out to the world.

*So looking back at the role and involvement of six different faiths in my journey, I developed a "love to all and hate to none" philosophy, because every faith has contributed to who am I today. It's become my duty to help the world without looking at age, sex, faith, or race, and just helping humanity*

93

*has made my life so much easier. Humanity has become my faith. So thank you to the world and thank you to Mother Earth;, we are a global family.*

## Toastmasters

After I moved to Canada, got an IT job, got married, and had my first son, life was good, but I felt like something was missing. I felt a little restless and stagnant, and then I realized that I needed to tell my stories from the stage. However, I had difficulty speaking in front of an audience; not only that, I had so many other speaking issues like poor diction, poor pronunciation, poor grammar, and speaking too fast. As they say, when the student is ready, the teacher will appear, and one day while standing in line for coffee I saw an ad that said "We create leaders". That ad was for Toastmasters—I walked in as a guest and delivered my very first Table Topics speech and won it.

The Downsview Toastmasters and all my fellow members gave me the confidence to speak in public and share my journey with the world. So thank you, Toastmasters, for giving me the voice to speak with confidence, which allowed me to quit my IT job and become a full-time business coach (https://www.coachrakesh.com) and motivational speaker. Special mention and thanks to my fellow Downsview Toastmasters friends; I would like to name a few of them here: Jake, Carmena, Larsen, Victor, and Rajesh.

## Slumdog Millionaire Movie

After I moved to Canada, I developed a fascination with listening to great motivators and speakers like Les Brown, Zig Ziglar, Tony Robbins, and Jim Rohn. I realized that the Western world gives a lot of importance to stories, and I became excited to share my own stories. But then I got frightened by the thought that if I shared my life stories that were full of poverty and struggle, people might not like me. That was until this movie came to my rescue.

*Slumdog Millionaire* was released in 2008 and won eight Oscars. I went to see it and realized that I had lived and experienced most parts of the movie, which gave me the confidence to share my stories. So thanks to director Danny Boyle and the movie *Slumdog Millionaire* for inspiring me, otherwise this book had no chance of coming into existence.

### The United States of America

I had heard a lot about America, but when I landed in San Francisco in 2008 and spent some time there, the one thing America taught me was to think big. It's all about thinking big, and that was when the seed was planted in me. Whatever success I have achieved, credit goes to that "thinking big" attitude, which I learned from America.

It's been almost twenty years that I've lived in Canada, but I will make sure to make two trips back to the USA— one pleasure trip with my family and one business trip to attend a conference that will be key for my professional advancement. So thanks to the United States of America for transforming my attitude from scarcity to abundance.

## Two Books:

### *Think & Grow Rich* by Napoleon Hill

This book was the very first personal development book I read after I got into the job market, and it changed my life forever. It has become the Bible of my personal prosperity. It's been almost twenty-five years since I was introduced to this gem, and I make sure that every birthday I listen to it without fail.

I learned many things from this book, but the most important lesson I learned was how to THINK. From then on I started thinking and reflecting about my life on a weekly (fifteen minutes), monthly (sixty minutes), quarterly (two hours), and yearly (one full day) basis to plan and execute. So thanks to this treasure. I highly recommend it to anyone and everyone.

### *The Magic of Thinking Big* by David J. Schwartz

*Thinking Big*, like *Think & Grow Rich*, is another gem that equally helped me to transform my personal growth and learn a lot. Just as *Think & Grow Rich* taught me to THINK, this one taught me to THINK BIG.

In addition to thinking big and so many other teachings, one very important lesson I learned at that young age (my early twenties) was the concept of not focusing on saving money but instead focusing on finding more streams of income. If you do not have any bad habits like gambling, drugs, alcohol, and wrong associations, then you will be saving money that could instead benefit you and your family So thanks to *The Magic of Thinking Big.*

Thank you to all the amazing friends with whom I have worked in the past twenty-five-plus years. Each of them has had a great impact on my life and supported and encouraged me to move forward.

Thank you to all my students that I have had the honor of teaching over the years. I am very proud of each of my kids. There are so many others who have been part of my journey, and I want to thank anyone and everyone who has inspired me and taught me life's lesson.

And finally...

Thank YOU, the reader, for investing your time reading this book.

# Contact Information

>>Tap here to see why you should consider booking Coach Rakesh for your campus or organization.<<

Coach Rakesh can be reached at Rakesh@CoachRakesh.com

Website: https://www.coachrakesh.com

Coaching, Consulting, and Speaking Services

www.CoachRakesh.com

Join our Facebook Group Freedom Lifestyle Design With Coach Rakesh

Follow Rakesh on Instagram

Follow Rakesh on Twitter

# Feedback Request

Please leave a review for my book, as I would greatly appreciate your feedback.

If for some reason you did not enjoy the book, then please contact me at Rakesh@CoachRakesh.com to discuss options prior to leaving a negative review, and please feel free to let me know how the book can be improved.